We rarely jump on our own – we pay more attention to organising people and being on time – we use larger aircraft, more altitude and we travel more.

Our gear weighs half as much, performs three times as well and has quadrupled in price – and – we're happy with the bargain it is.

We have people running off mountains, walking on parachutes and standing on formations.

We have formations docking with formations – even formations docking with people standing on formations. It somehow seems more difficult to believe than to do –

We're thinking about that too!

Our parachuting authorities show the same disinclination to each other that our governments do – but political insulation is perforated by friendships made between jumpers at International Competitions and while some countries will see this book as propaganda, there will be jumpers in those countries who will see it as 'the state of the art of jumping.'

SKIES CALL 2

PHOTOGRAPHERS:

ANDY KEECH · BILL PARSON · BOB WALTZER
BRAD GASTON · CARL BOENISH · CHARLIE McGURR
DANNY HUPERT · DAVE WATERMAN · 'FRENCHY' COURTOIS
GUY SAUVAGE · JASON NAULT · JEAN-PIERRE BOLLE
JERRY IRWIN · MAX DERETA · MICHEL AUVRAY
MIKE MOUNT · PAUL PROCTOR · PETER BOTTGENBACH
PHIL ROGGE · RAY COTTINGHAM · TOMMY DUNN

Man small
Why fall?
Skies call
That's all

SKIES CALL 2

PUBLISHED BY
ANDY KEECH.

DESIGNED AND
PRODUCED BY
J. PARTINGTON SMITH.

PUBLISHED IN ENGLAND.
© COPYRIGHT · ANDREW C. KEECH
FIRST EDITION MARCH 1979
Second printing October 1981
ISBN   0 950334 11 1

Printed by: Libra Offset Limited, London
Colour Separations by: Librascan Limited, London.

The years following the original "Skies Call" were not all that I expected. While I enjoyed the recognition and acceptance from my fellow jumpers, I was not prepared for my reaction to the friendly, frequently asked question "When are you putting out the next book?" An undertaking as large as this, though wonderfully exhilarating, is not entered into lightly for reasons I was especially aware of.

The first book took five years of loyal support by my wife, Marie.

What was possible, the first time, through ignorance, was unacceptable in terms of personal investment the second time around.

Photography is the blend of two ingredients, luck, and being there. The men who were there are listed opposite the appropriate frame number at the back of the book. Some people believe you make your own luck, in which case no further credit need be made.

I am indebted to the members of the 'Know Sense' Canopy RW team, Permutations, The US Army 8 man team, the Raeford RW Group, and the Pelican Starship team. It is a rare privilege to work with professional teams by International standards.

On a more personal level I would like to thank the unnamed openhearted souls who volunteered more time, talent and travel than could be sensibly accounted for. During the shoots that went into this book I found this generously demonstrated by Ed Christy, Jerry Jackson, Dennis Lynch and his exceptional parents.

I am particularly thankful for the assistance and guidance of Paul Reed, who built the camera mounts used on my projects. Paul orchestrated people and events to come together before the lens, kept me on schedule, and allowed me the comfort and reassurance of a capable, amusing friend.

The book is possible because of all this help, (and all those people out there who make Duct Tape!).

— ANDY KEECH

The first book was followed by an explosive increase in interesting activity throughout our Sport that called for photography.

The subject is international and the idea of involving photographers from all over the world seemed the obvious solution to a task as large as this was in our eyes.

It would provide us with the luxury of access, to the artistic eye of photographers who are household names in International parachuting, - and those with the potential.

— JPS

5

"That's relative workers for you . . .
crank up the engines
and they start dirt-diving!"

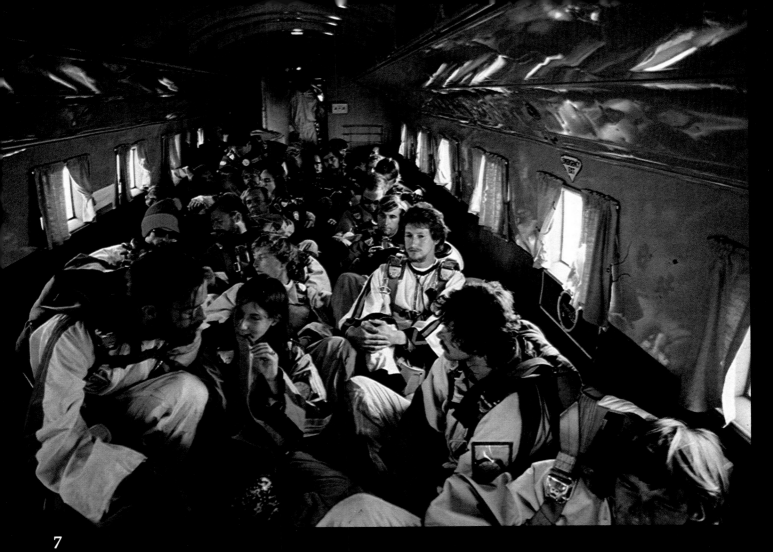

7

8

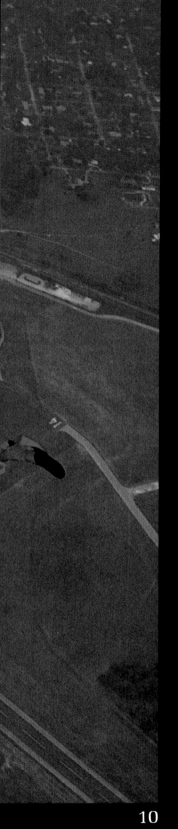

10   11

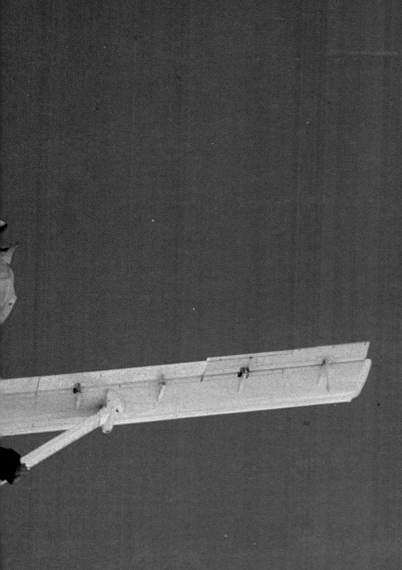

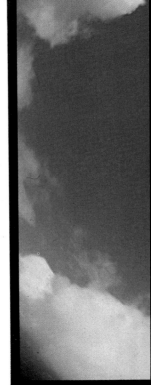

14

15

16

17

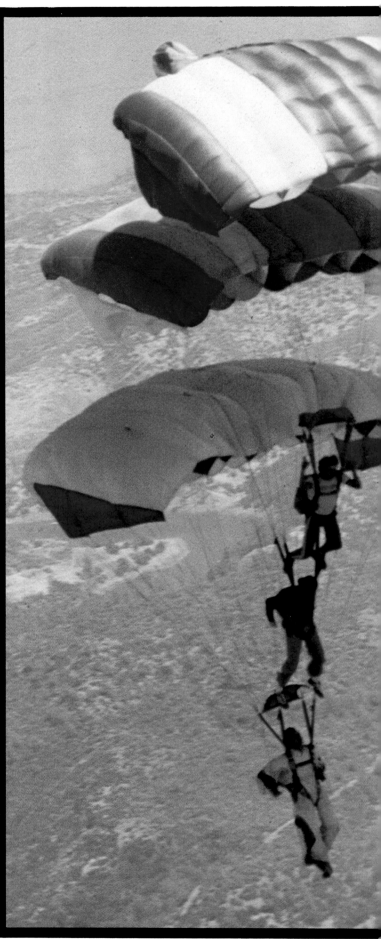

52

53

82

83

84

85

95

96

Canopy Relative Work (CRW), flying parachutes in formation and in contact must be the most graceful, fun, and unlikely happening in Skydiving in the Seventies.

Parachutists developed the 'Square' ram air parachute for fine control and precision accuracy landings on target.

Skydivers adopted this canopy because its long glide range could easily neutralise displacement errors in exiting at much higher altitudes.

The period of free fall, to the Skydiver, is the main point and purpose of the 'dive' – the canopy ride is merely the safest way to return to the ground.

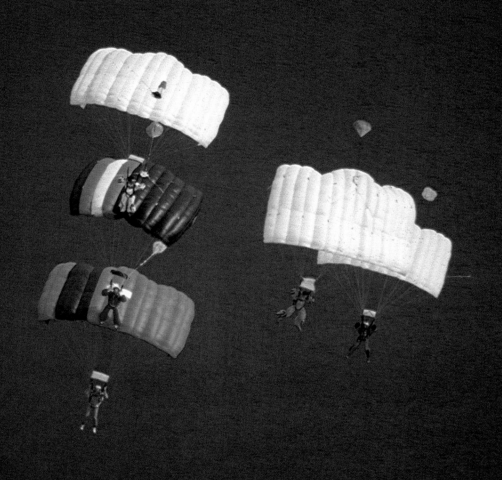

It may be one of the contradictions of our sport that the only significant development in the use of parachutes in 20 years came from Skydivers playing together after opening.

It must be years before we see where CRW goes. Canopy stacks are sensitive to thermals, and this single point may make competition unequal and unfair to teams jumping in the heat of the afternoon – so long as rules of competition prevent it becoming a trade off between safety and high scores, canopy RW is the big event of the future, and will surely influence parachute design and improve our understanding of the equipment we otherwise give little attention to. We will become, more and more, the parachute pilots our common sense and the parachute manufacturers have been advising us to be.

We now have a different way to use altitude, and for much longer periods of time. Conversations between jumpers in the air, the feel of a live open parachute, are new and novel experiences to us.

CRW is still largely a
4 dimensional mystery,
potentially dangerous
because we don't understand
very much of its physics,
but especially interesting to
the curious, advanced jumper.
The next few years will
show most of the potential
of CRW and it will then
be seen in its full colours.

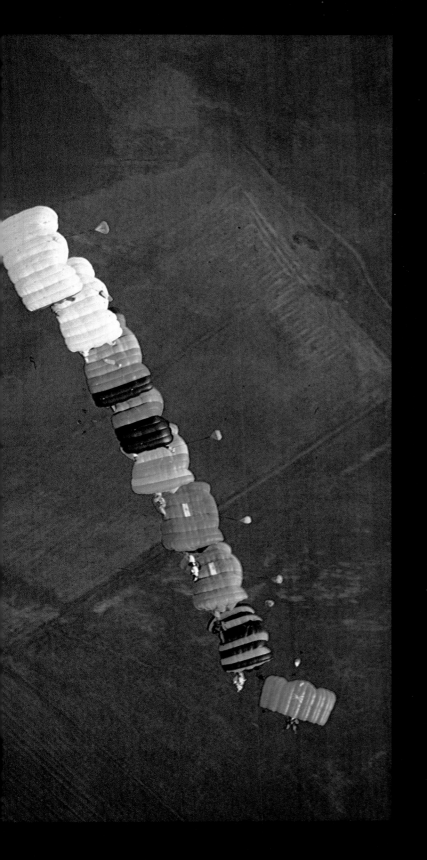

107

108

117

118

125

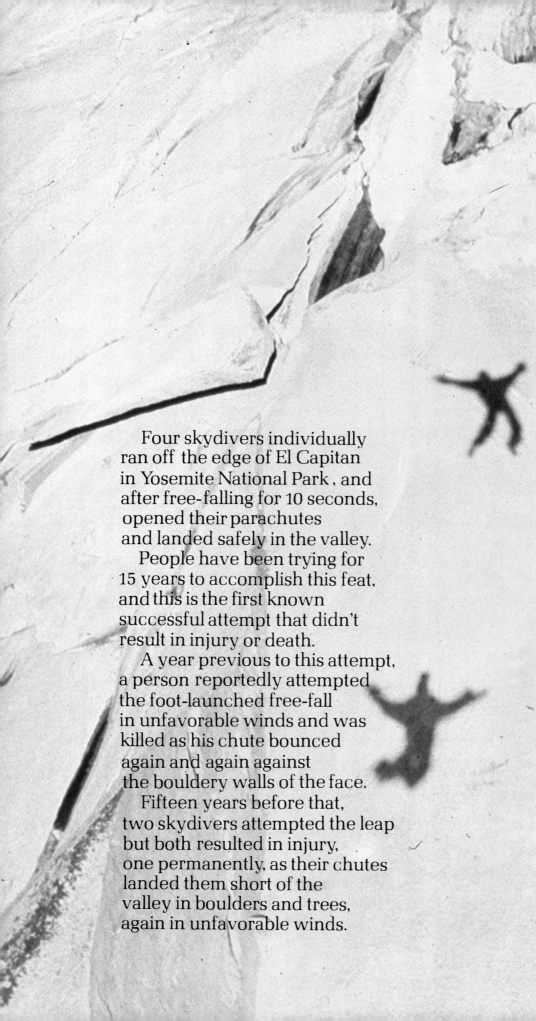

Four skydivers individually
ran off the edge of El Capitan
in Yosemite National Park, and
after free-falling for 10 seconds,
opened their parachutes
and landed safely in the valley.
People have been trying for
15 years to accomplish this feat,
and this is the first known
successful attempt that didn't
result in injury or death.
A year previous to this attempt,
a person reportedly attempted
the foot-launched free-fall
in unfavorable winds and was
killed as his chute bounced
again and again against
the bouldery walls of the face.
Fifteen years before that,
two skydivers attempted the leap
but both resulted in injury,
one permanently, as their chutes
landed them short of the
valley in boulders and trees,
again in unfavorable winds.

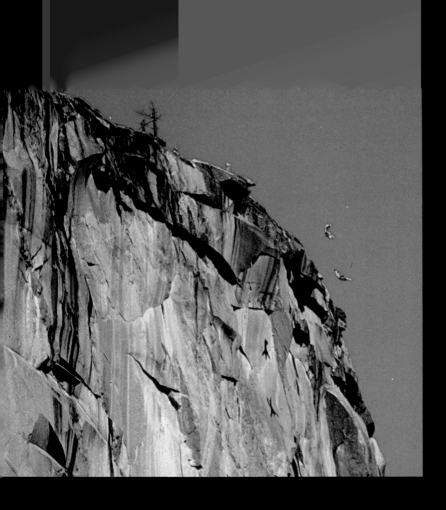

Three important factors contributed
to the safety and success of the jumps.
    First was not having the attitude,
"I've hiked all this way and I'm not about
to hike back down without making this
jump, regardless of the winds."
    Another was the thorough mastery
of the sky-diver's "track" position
which enables him to move forward
across the ground at speeds of
up to 90 feet per second (60 mph).
    The third factor was the use
of the recently developed "square" or
ram air parachute which has a lot of
forward speed developed by its airfoil
cross-section shape, outgliding a round
parachute by three to one.

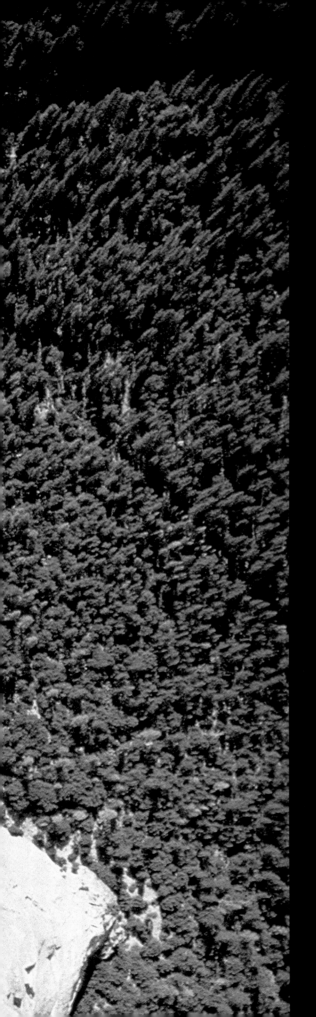

The four jumps culminated two
months of constant training, including
cliff diving into water, balloon jumping,
five trips to Yosemite totalling
14 days of back-packing.
Patience and respect for El Capitan
and the weather remained uppermost
in everyone's minds.
Radio communication ensured
good ground winds (zero ground winds)
and lack of congestion at the landing site.

Prior to the jumps, the biggest fear
the jumpers had was opening their
chutes too near the wall and running
into it, probably collapsing their chutes.
With modern skydiving techniques
and the latest light-weight parachute gear,
it was demonstrated that almost
500 feet of separation between jumper
and cliff is attainable.
With this new break-through
in knowledge, there are hundreds of
qualified skydivers who could
successfully accomplish the feat.
The feat was accomplished – not as a
stunt or to seek publicity, but to expand
man's dominion over his environment and
pave the way for future jumps.
The Park Service will probably choose
initially to monitor future jumps, just as
they presently do for all hang-glider
flights in the park, and just as they used
to do for all major rock-climbing assaults,
to ensure jumper qualifications are met
and perfect weather conditions
are present.

Hopefully cliff jumping can be
recognized as a new sport – complete
with exhibitions and competitions, as
commonplace and publicly accepted
as rock climbing has become.

El Capitan is currently the only known
safe place in the United States from
which to perform a cliff jump.

Cliff jumping is exhilarating,
beautiful to make and to watch, and can
be done harmoniously with nature,
ecology, and society.

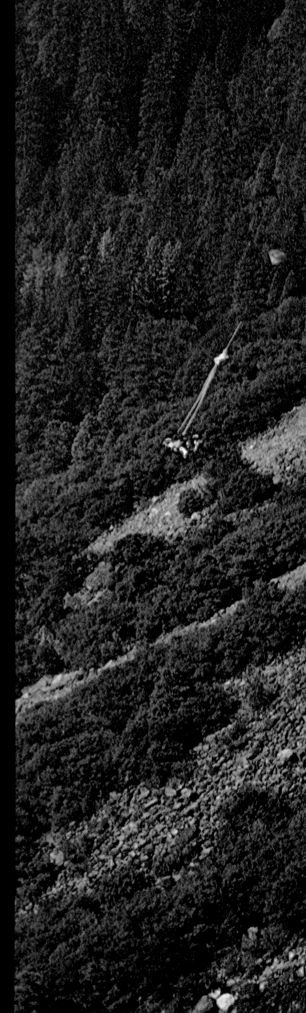

137

142

143

Progress — turning better ideas into actions is the ongoing constant of our sport — it comes directly from our people, the subjects of these pictures.

If they felt satisfaction in doing the exceptional and just half the fun that th company was to their photographers, th had a good time. We had a good time to we'd like to do it again.